The Science of Living Things

What is an Elephant?

John Crossingham & Bobbie Kalman

🌱 Crabtree Publishing Company

www.crabtreebooks.com

The Science of Living Things Series
A Bobbie Kalman Book

Dedicated by John Crossingham
For Candis Steenbergen,
the strongest, toughest, rarest, most noble animal I know

Editor-in-Chief
Bobbie Kalman

Writing team
John Crossingham
Bobbie Kalman

Editors
Niki Walker
Amanda Bishop
Kathryn Smithyman

Cover design
Kymberley McKee Murphy

Computer design
Margaret Amy Reiach

Production coordinator
Heather Fitzpatrick

Photo researcher
Heather Fitzpatrick

Consultant
Patricia Loesche, Ph.D., Animal Behavior Program,
Department of Psychology, University of Washington

Illustrations
Barbara Bedell: page 7 (bottom), 10
Bonna Rouse: page 6, 7 (right, left, and center), 11, 20, 21, 25, 28

Photographs
Frank S. Balthis: pages 10, 21, 23 (bottom), 30
Wolfgang Kaehler: pages 14, 15 (bottom), 19 (top), 25, 28,
    29 (bottom)
Robert McCaw: page 19 (bottom)
Tom Stack and Associates: Barbara Gerlach: page 24 (top);
    Thomas Kitchin: page 29 (top);
    Spencer Swanger: page 20
Michael P. Turco: page 23 (top)
Other images by Adobe Image Library, Digital Stock,
    and Digital Vision

Crabtree Publishing Company

www.crabtreebooks.com   1-800-387-7650

PMB 16A
350 Fifth Avenue
Suite 3308
New York, NY
10118

612 Welland Avenue
St. Catharines
Ontario
Canada
L2M 5V6

73 Lime Walk
Headington
Oxford
OX3 7AD
United Kingdom

Cataloging in Publication Data
Crossingham, John
    What is an elephant? / John Crossingham & Bobbie Kalman.
    p. cm. -- (The science of living things)
    Includes index.
    Describes the physical characteristics, behavior, life
cycle, and looks at the dangers facing elephants today.
    ISBN 0-86505-989-6 (RLB) -- ISBN 0-86505-966-7 (pbk.)
    1. Elephants--Juvenile literature. [1. Elephants.]   I. Kalman,
Bobbie. II. Title. III. Series.
    QL737.P98 C76 2002
    599.67--dc21
                                        2001047103

Contents

Elephants

Elephants are the largest and heaviest land animals on Earth. They are **mammals**. Like other mammals, they are **warm-blooded**, which means that their body temperature stays the same in hot or cold surroundings. Male elephants are called **bulls**, and females are called **cows**. Cows give birth to live babies called **calves**. Their bodies make milk for the calves to drink.

Gentle giants

Elephants are among the strongest animals on the planet. Despite their size and strength, they are gentle, intelligent, and affectionate. They rarely fight, even when they are defending themselves against enemies. Instead, elephants charge at their attackers and often turn away at the last moment. Elephants live and travel in large family groups called **herds**. They form strong bonds with the members of their group. Female elephants stay with the same group until they die.

Long life

Elephants are well protected by their large size and by the members of their herd. Most elephants have a **life span** of 60 years, but some live more than 70 years. They live almost as long as humans do!

Elephant family tree

There are two **species**, or types, of elephants living today—the African elephant and the Asian elephant. Each species is named after the continent on which it lives. Elephants are sometimes called **pachyderms**, which comes from a Greek word meaning "tough skin." Elephants belong to the order *Proboscidea* and the family *Elephantidae*.

Platybelodon, an early cousin, lived about 25 million years ago.

Ancient relatives

Millions of years ago, Earth was full of animals similar to elephants. The first **ancestors**, or early relatives, of elephants were smaller and had different tusks. Platybelodon, above, had flat tusks that grew out of its bottom lip.

*Woolly mammoths are the most recent elephant ancestors to become **extinct**, or to die off. They disappeared about 10 000 years ago.*

African elephants

African elephants are the largest elephants. They are found in many African countries, including Zaire, South Africa, Namibia, Botswana, and Zimbabwe. The adult elephants are about eleven feet (3.4 m) tall and weigh seven tons (6350 kg).

Asian elephants

Asian elephants live in forests in India, Nepal, Sumatra, Sri Lanka, and Thailand. They are also known as Indian elephants. Asian elephants are slightly smaller than African elephants. Adults are about ten feet (3 m) tall and weigh about six tons (5443 kg).

Tiny relative

The hyrax is a small, furry animal. Although it looks nothing like the giant elephant, this mammal has a similar bone structure to that of an elephant. Scientists believe that the hyrax and the elephant share a common ancestor.

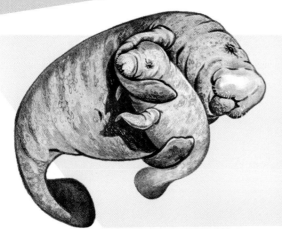

Water cousins

Dugongs and manatees are also related to elephants. These large mammals live in the sea and spend most of their time eating plants.

An elephant's body

Elephants live in hot climates and spend most of the day eating. Their bodies are perfectly **adapted**, or suited, to their **habitats** and lifestyles. Their large ears, wrinkled skin, and long tusks help them survive.

An elephant has poor eyesight and cannot see far ahead. It also cannot see behind itself. As a result, the elephant relies mainly on its senses of smell, hearing, and touch.

An elephant can lift objects with its tusks. Some elephants also use them to dig for food and water.

The trunk is very flexible because it has no bones. It can lift objects and is also used for smelling, drinking, and moving food to the elephant's mouth.

Big fans

Although an elephant has excellent hearing, its ears are large for a different reason—they help keep the elephant cool. An elephant cannot sweat. Instead, warm blood travels through veins in the back of its ears. These veins are very close to the skin's surface. They release heat into the air through the skin. Doing so cools the blood and, as a result, the rest of the elephant's body. An elephant also flaps its ears like fans to move cool air against its back.

An elephant uses its tail as a fly swatter on areas of its body that its trunk cannot reach. Most of the elephant's body is hairless, but the tail has long hairs that are perfect for swatting insects.

The bottom of an elephant's foot is soft and spongy, allowing the heavy animal to walk quietly.

An elephant's skin is one inch (2.5 cm) thick and very tough. It protects the animal from insect bites. The skin is also wrinkled. The wrinkles trap water, which helps keep the elephant cool.

Tusks and teeth

An elephant's tusks are actually teeth called **incisors**. Many other animals have incisors, too, but they are not nearly as big! In fact, elephant tusks are the largest, heaviest animal teeth. Most tusks are about six feet (2 m) long and weigh about 50 pounds (23 kg) each.

Always growing

An elephant calf has small tusks that fall out after a year. These **milk teeth** are replaced by permanent tusks that will grow throughout the elephant's life. An adult's tusks are very strong and sturdy. They can lift over 2000 pounds (900 kg)!

Tools and weapons

Tusks are important for survival. When threatened by predators such as lions, elephants try to scare them away by pointing their tusks and charging. Elephants also dig with their tusks to find underground water or food when the weather is dry. The water they dig up is often shared by other animals such as zebras and wildebeests.

Ivory

Tusks are made of a material called **ivory**, which is very valuable to humans. Each year, many elephants are killed for their tusks. People use the ivory to make piano keys, sculptures, jewelry, and good-luck charms.

Other teeth

Tusks may be useful for digging up and carrying food, but they are not used for chewing. An elephant has four flat teeth called **molars** that it uses to crush and grind its food. The molars soften tough grasses and leaves so they can be **digested**. All this chewing wears down the molars, so an elephant grows six sets of them in its lifetime. It gets its final set around the age of 30. These teeth last about 30 years. When they wear out, the animal cannot chew its food, and it soon dies.

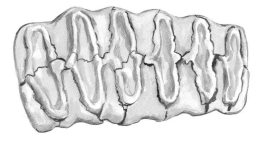

This elephant molar is old and cracked. A new molar has grown in its place.

Elephants are right- or left-tusked, just as people are right- or left-handed. An elephant's preferred tusk is often shorter than the other because of wear.

The trunk

An elephant's trunk is both its upper lip and its nose. The elephant uses it to smell, breathe, drink, bathe, lift food to its mouth, pick up objects, swat flies, and greet other elephants. The trunk is strong enough to pull a tree from the ground, but it can also do delicate jobs. Its tip has "fingers" that pluck grasses and leaves. The fingers can gently handle objects as small as coins!

Elephants use their trunks to reach leaves on tall trees.

Sense of touch

The tip of an elephant's trunk has an accurate sense of touch. The elephant can use it to judge the size, shape, texture, and temperature of objects. Elephants also use their trunks to caress one another.

Can you smell that?

Besides its sense of touch, an elephant relies heavily on its excellent sense of smell. It can memorize many scents and is able to recognize its young, other elephants, and its favorite foods by their smells. Its sense of smell also gives an elephant early warning of an approaching enemy. An elephant can smell humans over one mile (1.6 km) away. It catches scents by waving its trunk in the air.

Water hose

An elephant can also use its trunk like a hose. It sucks up water in its trunk to squirt into its mouth for a drink or spray over its body for a bath.

When a young elephant is nervous, it puts its trunk into an older elephant's mouth.

Food and water

Elephants grow as large as they do for a good reason—they spend up to 20 hours a day eating! Most elephants eat about 300 pounds (135 kg) of food a day. They are **herbivores**, which means they eat only plants. Their menu includes leaves, roots, grasses, and bark. Elephants especially love fruits such as dates, plums, and coconuts.

Elephants use their trunks to grab fruit and leaves from trees. When food is out of reach, they pull the tree right out of the ground. Sometimes they ram the tree to knock it down. After eating the leaves, they strip off the bark with their tusks and eat the bark as well. Elephants will even eat the wood of the tree.

Needing a lot of water

When water is available, an elephant will drink up to 50 gallons (200 L) a day. Elephants can go without water for three days if they have to. When a water source dries up, they will travel up to 80 miles (125 km) in search of a new one. Elephants also use their tusks to dig underground in search of water.

Mud bath!

Bathing is an important daily activity. Elephants are bothered by flies that land on their bodies and bite them. A bath washes off these pests. After bathing, an elephant rolls in mud and covers its body with dirt. When the mud dries, it protects the skin from new insect bites. The mud also traps moisture against the skin and helps keep the animal cool. Elephants sometimes spend hours wallowing in mud.

Elephants are never far away from water. They use it for drinking, bathing, and cooling down.

After bathing, an elephant uses its trunk to spray dirt on its body. The dirt protects its skin from insects and the sun.

Communication

Scientists are discovering that elephant communication is complex, like that of whales and dolphins. Elephants communicate with one another using touch, signs, and sounds, or **calls**. Elephants recognize one another by their voices because each one's voice is slightly different. When two related elephants meet, they greet one another happily with sounds and touches. If an elephant wants to be left alone, it lets other elephants know by raising its head and spreading its ears.

Big vocabulary

Elephants have about 25 different calls, each with a specific meaning. One of the most common elephant calls is the **contact rumble**. This rumble is so low that humans cannot hear it. It is called **infrasound**. Infrasound signals travel far—an elephant can hear another elephant rumbling over two miles (3.2 km) away. When an elephant wanders off to find food, it uses contact rumbles to stay in touch with its herd.

Elephants also make a loud, shrill cry called **trumpeting**. Trumpeting usually expresses fear or anger. Elephants trumpet to warn others that danger is present.

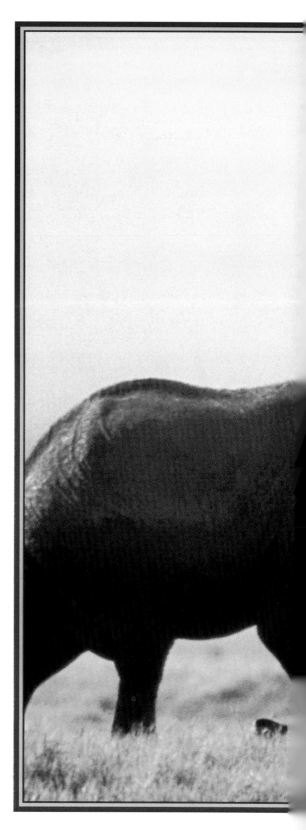

Good to see you!

"An elephant never forgets" is a popular expression. Although this saying is not quite true, elephants are intelligent and they do have excellent memories! They can remember one another even after spending several years apart. When two elephants that grew up together reunite, they rumble and wrap their trunks together. Sometimes they put the tips of their trunks into each other's mouths.

Social life

Elephants are **social** animals, which means they spend their lives with other elephants. Female elephants live in herds with their extended families. Most herds have five to twenty members. Some herds are made up of a mother, her daughters, and their young. Other herds include aunts and cousins, too.

A herd is led by a **matriarch**, or the oldest female. She knows everything the herd needs to know to survive, including travel routes and places to dig when water dries up. The matriarch passes on this information to the other cows. When she dies, one of the older cows becomes the new matriarch.

Elephants in a herd protect one another by forming a tight circle and pointing their tusks at predators.

No bulls in a herd

There are no bulls in a herd—only cows and calves. A male calf stays with the herd until he is 12 to 14 years old. After that age, the young bull lives on his own or in a small group of males called a **bull band**. The only time bulls and cows come together is during **mating season**, which is when they make babies.

Protective mothers

An elephant calf makes a tasty meal for predators such as lions and jackals. Cows are fiercely protective of their young. If a predator approaches, the cows circle around the calves and point their tusks at the enemy. If the predator does not leave, the cows charge at it and even stomp on it with their giant feet.

Mourning the loss

Mothers and calves are especially close, but all herd members are affectionate. If an elephant is dying, its herd does not leave. The other herd members try to lift the dying animal to its feet and bring it food and water. When the elephant dies, the others place grasses and branches over its body. Some elephants stay with a dead herd member for several days.

An elephant charges to protect her young. She holds her head high and spreads her ears wide.

An elephant visits her dead relatives. Vultures wait nearby to eat the carcasses.

19

On the road

Elephants walk in tight groups and rarely stray while traveling.

Elephants are **nomadic** animals—they do not stay long in one place. A herd travels within an area called a **range**, which can be thousands of square miles in size. The herd members follow the matriarch and wander the same routes year after year. By constantly moving, the elephants give plants in different grazing areas a chance to grow back. Their food and water will not run out if they keep moving from place to place.

Staying on their toes

Elephants are **digitigrade** animals, which means they walk on their toes. Doing so gives elephants excellent balance and turning ability. They usually walk at speeds between five and ten miles per hour (8 to 16 km/h). Despite their enormous size and weight, elephants can charge for a short distance at 25 miles per hour (40 km/h). Elephants have many grooves on the bottoms of their feet. The grooves grip the ground so the elephants will not slip and fall.

*An elephant's foot **contracts**, or becomes smaller, when the animal lifts it. This shrinkage allows the elephant to pull its feet out of deep, muddy footprints that would trap other animals.*

Elephants are strong swimmers and use their legs to paddle through water. In order to breathe, elephants hold their trunks like snorkels above the water's surface.

Mating

Mating season is the one time each year that bulls and cows live in the same area. This short season lasts about a week. Elephants take a long time to grow up and reach **maturity**, which is when they are ready to mate. Females begin mating when they are about 12 years old. Some males are not ready to mate until they are 20 years old.

*Bull elephants often test each other's strength. The strongest one is called the **dominant** bull. Dominant bulls mate more often than other males do.*

The time is right

In order to mate, a cow must be in a state called **estrus**. When she is in estrus, she gives off a special scent that bull elephants recognize. Estrus lasts only a few days each year.

They musth mate

Bulls also have a special state for mating, called **musth**. They have organs called **glands** on the sides of their heads. When a male is in musth, the glands swell and **secrete**, or produce, a liquid with a strong scent. Males do not have to be in musth to mate, but it is easier if they are. All males must compete with one another in order to mate with females. Bulls in musth are very aggressive and more likely to win the females.

A long wait

After mating, it takes a long time before the calf is born. The baby **gestates**, or grows inside its mother's body, for 22 months—that is almost two years! This gestation period is so long that most females give birth only once every four or five years.

This photograph shows a male elephant's musth gland secreting liquid.

*After a pair has mated, the cows have a **mating pandemonium**. They trumpet, shake their ears, and touch the pair with their trunks.*

Baby elephants

A calf uses its trunk to suck milk, which it then shoots into its mouth. It also uses its trunk to pick up objects such as sticks.

Cows usually give birth to one calf at a time, but some mothers do have twins. Calves are very attached to their mothers. Females stay with their herds for life, and male calves stay with their mothers until they are between 12 and 14 years old.

Mother's milk

A calf weighs about 250 pounds (115 kg) and stands over three feet (1 m) tall. A newborn calf drinks milk from its mother's body. It drinks up to three gallons (11 L) a day! Calves start eating plants after about four months but continue to drink milk for up to ten years.

I can walk

Elephant herds are always on the move looking for food. A calf can keep up with its herd because it is able to walk an hour after it is born. Alone, a newborn calf is an easy target for lions, tigers, or jackals. By staying with the herd, the calf is protected by its mother and the other elephants.

(right) A newborn calf has tiny hairs on its head.
(below) Calves need protection from predators.

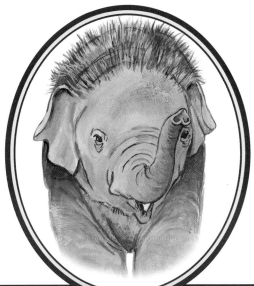

African elephants

The African elephant has a dip in its back, and its forehead is flat. It has rings all the way down its trunk, with two fingers at the tip for grasping. Its ears are large and wide. Some people say they are shaped like the continent of Africa. The African elephant lives in a hot, dry climate and needs large ears to cool off its body.

Two habitats

African elephants live south of the Sahara Desert in Africa. The terrain is covered by thick forests and flat grasslands called **savannahs**. Elephants that live in forests are slightly different from those that live on the grasslands, but they are all African elephants.

Smaller spaces, smaller bodies

The African elephant of the forest has a slightly smaller body and tusks than the African elephant of the savannah. Trees grow close together in the forest, and having a smaller body allows a forest elephant to move among the trees more easily than a savannah elephant could.

Asian elephants

Asian elephants have smaller ears than African elephants have.

Asian elephants are slightly different from their bigger African cousins. The Asian elephant has a humped forehead, a rounded back, and a trunk with only one finger. Asian elephants have smoother skin, and some are a lighter gray color. They sometimes have colored blotches on their skin.

It's a jungle out there!

Many of the differences between Asian and African elephants have to do with their habitats. African elephants live in hot and dry surroundings, but Asian elephants live in moist jungle habitats. Water is more plentiful in the jungle, and the thick forests are full of vegetation. Asian elephants do not need wrinkled skin to trap moisture or large ears to use as fans. Unlike African elephants, Asian elephants seldom need to dig for food.

Where are your tusks?

Only male Asian elephants have visible tusks, and not all males grow them. Tuskless males are larger than males with tusks. A female's tusks, or **tushes**, are so short that they usually do not grow past her lip.

Hard workers

In India, people use Asian elephants for transportation and work. At logging camps, elephants move logs and knock down trees. Each elephant is cared for by a trainer called a **mahout**. At the end of the day, the mahout takes the elephant to a stream and bathes it by hand.

This female's tushes grow just past her lip.

An elephant enjoys a bath after a hard day's work.

In danger

Elephants are so large and strong that they have few natural enemies. Even lions and tigers have a hard time killing adult elephants. Humans are the number one killers of elephants.

The ivory trade

Since early times, people have killed elephants for their tusks. Before people had guns, they could kill only a few elephants. In the 1970s, however, powerful automatic guns became available. Illegal hunters called **poachers** easily killed elephants with these guns. At this time, ivory became very valuable, so poachers killed as many elephants as they could. By the end of the 1980s, the number of elephants in Africa dropped from 1,300,000 to 600,000. The Asian elephant population fell to fewer than 44,000.

Banning ivory

In 1989, the United Nations Convention on International Trade in Endangered Species (CITES) recognized that elephants were in danger of disappearing. The group, made up of 115 countries, agreed to stop, or **ban**, the sale of ivory between countries.

Too many elephants?

While elephants were **endangered** in most countries, Botswana, Namibia, and Zimbabwe had so many that the elephants were running out of space. They destroyed crops and sometimes injured people. The governments had to **cull** herds, or kill some elephants to keep the population under control. The governments wanted to sell the ivory from these culled elephants.

Some people think that tourism is the best way for African countries to make money from elephants. What do you think?

The countries argued that their elephants were not endangered, and their people needed money. They promised to use part of the profit for elephant **conservation**. In 1997, CITES allowed the three countries to sell their ivory.

More problems

Poachers were able to sneak illegal ivory into Botswana, Namibia, and Zimbabwe because it is difficult to tell from which country ivory comes. As a result, poaching increased.

An uncertain future

In 2000, the countries of Africa agreed to stop trading ivory, but this decision may change in the future. People are still killing elephants, even though it is **illegal**, or against the law. You can learn more about elephants and ivory on the Internet. Start at the Elephant Information Repository (http://elephant.elehost.com).

Glossary

ancestor An early animal from which later species developed

calf A baby elephant

conservation The planned protection and management of an animal species or habitat to prevent its destruction or disappearance

cow An adult female elephant

digest To break down food into a form the body can absorb

endangered Describing an animal or plant species that is in danger of dying out

habitat The place where an animal naturally lives

herd A group of elephants made up of female relatives and their young

life span The average length of time a type of animal lives

mammal A type of warm-blooded animal that has a backbone, some hair or fur, and that feeds its young with milk made in its body

mate To join together to make babies

mating season The time of year when male and female animals mate

Index

1 2 3 4 5 6 7 8 9 0   Printed in the U.S.A.   0 9 8 7 6 5 4 3 2